I0472945

Materials Handling and Storing

U.S. Department of Labor

Occupational Safety and Health Administration

OSHA 2236
2002 (Revised)

Contents

Introduction

Handling and storing materials involve diverse operations such as hoisting tons of steel with a crane; driving a truck loaded with concrete blocks; carrying bags or materials manually; and stacking palletized bricks or other materials such as drums, barrels, kegs, and lumber.

The efficient handling and storing of materials are vital to industry. In addition to raw materials, these operations provide a continuous flow of parts and assemblies through the workplace and ensure that materials are available when needed. Unfortunately, the improper handling and storing of materials often result in costly injuries.

What should your employees know before moving, handling, and storing materials?

In addition to training and education, applying general safety principles—such as proper work practices, equipment, and controls—can help reduce workplace accidents involving the moving, handling, and storing of materials. Whether moving materials manually or mechanically, your employees should know and understand the potential hazards associated with the task at hand and how to control their workplaces to minimize the danger.

Because numerous injuries can result from improperly handling and storing materials, workers should also be aware of accidents that may result from the unsafe or improper handling of equipment as well as from improper work practices. In addition, workers should be able to recognize the methods for eliminating—or at least minimizing—the occurrence of such accidents. Employers and employees should examine their workplaces to detect any unsafe or unhealthful conditions, practices, or equipment and take corrective action.

What are the potential hazards for workers?

Workers frequently cite the weight and bulkiness of objects that they lift as major contributing factors to their injuries. In 1999, for example, more than 420,000 workplace accidents resulted in back injuries. Bending, followed by twisting and turning, were the more commonly cited movements that caused back injuries.

Other hazards include falling objects, improperly stacked materials, and various types of equipment. You should make your employees aware of potential injuries that can occur when manually moving materials, including the following:

- Strains and sprains from lifting loads improperly or from carrying loads that are either too large or too heavy,

- Fractures and bruises caused by being struck by materials or by being caught in pinch points, and

- Cuts and bruises caused by falling materials that have been improperly stored or by incorrectly cutting ties or other securing devices.

What precautions should workers take when moving materials manually?

When moving materials manually, workers should attach handles or holders to loads. In addition, workers should always wear appropriate personal protective equipment and use proper lifting techniques. To prevent injury from oversize loads, workers should seek help in the following:

- When a load is so bulky that employees cannot properly grasp or lift it,

- When employees cannot see around or over a load, or

- When employees cannot safely handle a load.

Using the following personal protective equipment prevents needless injuries when manually moving materials:

- Hand and forearm protection, such as gloves, for loads with sharp or rough edges.

- Eye protection.

- Steel-toed safety shoes or boots.

- Metal, fiber, or plastic metatarsal guards to protect the instep area from impact or compression.

See OSHA's booklet, *Personal Protective Equipment* (OSHA 3077), for additional information.

Employees should use blocking materials to manage loads safely. Workers should also be cautious when placing blocks under a raised load to ensure that the load is not released before removing their hands from under the load. Blocking materials and timbers should be large and strong enough to support the load safely. In addition to materials with cracks, workers should not use materials with rounded corners, splintered pieces, or dry rot for blocking.

What precautions should workers take when moving materials mechanically?

Using mechanical equipment to move and store materials increases the potential for employee injuries. Workers must be aware of both manual handling safety concerns and safe equipment operating techniques. Employees should avoid overloading equipment when moving materials mechanically by letting the weight, size, and shape of the material being moved dictate the type of equipment used. All materials-handling equipment has rated capacities that determine the maximum weight the equipment can safely handle and the conditions under which it can handle that weight. Employers must ensure that the equipment-rated capacity is displayed on each piece of equipment and is not exceeded except for load testing.

Although workers may be knowledgeable about powered equipment, they should take precautions when stacking and storing material. When picking up items with a powered industrial truck, workers must do the following:

- Center the load on the forks as close to the mast as possible to minimize the potential for the truck tipping or the load falling,

- Avoid overloading a lift truck because it impairs control and causes tipping over,

- Do not place extra weight on the rear of a counterbalanced forklift to allow an overload,

- Adjust the load to the lowest position when traveling,

- Follow the truck manufacturer's operational requirements, and

- Pile and cross-tier all stacked loads correctly when possible.

What precautions must workers take to avoid storage hazards?

Stored materials must not create a hazard for employees. Employers should make workers aware of such factors as the materials' height and weight, how accessible the stored materials are to the user, and the condition of the containers where the materials are being stored when stacking and piling materials. To prevent creating hazards when storing materials, employers must do the following:

- Keep storage areas free from accumulated materials that cause tripping, fires, or explosions, or that may contribute to the harboring of rats and other pests;

- Place stored materials inside buildings that are under construction and at least 6 feet from hoist ways, or inside floor openings and at least 10 feet away from exterior walls;

- Separate noncompatible material; and

- Equip employees who work on stored grain in silos, hoppers, or tanks, with lifelines and safety belts.

  In addition, workers should consider placing bound material on racks, and secure it by stacking, blocking, or interlocking to prevent it from sliding, falling, or collapsing.

What safeguards must workers follow when stacking materials?

  Stacking materials can be dangerous if workers do not follow safety guidelines. Falling materials and collapsing loads can crush or pin workers, causing injuries or death. To help prevent injuries when stacking materials, workers must do the following:

- Stack lumber no more than 16 feet high if it is handled manually, and no more than 20 feet if using a forklift;

- Remove all nails from used lumber before stacking;

- Stack and level lumber on solidly supported bracing;

- Ensure that stacks are stable and self-supporting;

- Do not store pipes and bars in racks that face main aisles to avoid creating a hazard to passersby when removing supplies;

- Stack bags and bundles in interlocking rows to keep them secure; and

- Stack bagged material by stepping back the layers and cross-keying the bags at least every ten layers (to remove bags from the stack, start from the top row first).

During materials stacking activities, workers must also do the following:

- Store baled paper and rags inside a building no closer than 18 inches to the walls, partitions, or sprinkler heads;

- Band boxed materials or secure them with cross-ties or shrink plastic fiber;

- Stack drums, barrels, and kegs symmetrically;

- Block the bottom tiers of drums, barrels, and kegs to keep them from rolling if stored on their sides;

- Place planks, sheets of plywood dunnage, or pallets between each tier of drums, barrels, and kegs to make a firm, flat, stacking surface when stacking on end;

- Chock the bottom tier of drums, barrels, and kegs on each side to prevent shifting in either direction when stacking two or more tiers high; and

- Stack and block poles as well as structural steel, bar stock, and other cylindrical materials to prevent spreading or tilting unless they are in racks.

In addition, workers should do the following:

- Paint walls or posts with stripes to indicate maximum stacking heights for quick reference;

- Observe height limitations when stacking materials;

- Consider the need for availability of the material; and

- Stack loose bricks no more than 7 feet in height. (When these stacks reach a height of 4 feet, taper them back 2 inches for every foot of height above the 4-foot level. When masonry blocks are stacked higher than 6 feet, taper the stacks back one-half block for each tier above the 6-foot level.)

Important Safety Measures

To reduce the number of accidents associated with workplace equipment, employers must train employees in the proper use and limitations of the equipment they operate. In addition to powered industrial trucks, this includes knowing how to safely and effectively use equipment such as conveyors, cranes, and slings.

What safety measures should employers take regarding conveyors?

When using conveyors, workers may get their hands caught in nip points where the conveyor medium runs near the frame or over support members or rollers. Workers also may be struck by material falling off the conveyor, or they may get caught in the conveyor and drawn into the conveyor path as a result. To prevent or reduce the severity of an injury, employers must take the following precautions to protect workers:

- Install an emergency button or pull cord designed to stop the conveyor at the employee's work station.

- Install emergency stop cables that extend the entire length of continuously accessible conveyor belts so that the cables can be accessed from any location along the conveyor.

- Design the emergency stop switch so that it must be reset before the conveyor can be restarted.

- Ensure that appropriate personnel inspect the conveyor and clear the stoppage before restarting a conveyor that has stopped due to an overload.

- Prohibit employees from riding on a materials-handling conveyor.

- Provide guards where conveyors pass over work areas or aisles to keep employees from being struck by falling material. (If the crossover is low enough for workers to run into it, mark the guard with a warning sign or paint it a bright color to protect employees.)

- Cover screw conveyors completely except at loading and discharging points. (At those points, guards must protect employees against contacting the moving screw. The guards are movable, and they must be interlocked to prevent conveyor movement when the guards are not in place.)

What safety measures should employers take regarding cranes?

Employers must permit only thoroughly trained and competent workers to operate cranes. Operators should know what they are lifting and what it weighs. For example, the rated capacity of mobile cranes varies with the length of the boom and the boom radius. When a crane has a telescoping boom, a load may be safe to lift at a short boom length or a short boom radius, but may overload the crane when the boom is extended and the radius increases.

To reduce the severity of an injury, employers must take the following precautions:

- Equip all cranes that have adjustable booms with boom angle indicators.

- Provide cranes with telescoping booms with some means to determine boom lengths unless the load rating is independent of the boom length.

- Post load rating charts in the cab of cab-operated cranes. (All cranes do not have uniform capacities for the same boom length and radius in all directions around the chassis of the vehicle.)

- Require workers to always check the crane's load chart to ensure that the crane will not be overloaded by operating conditions.

- Instruct workers to plan lifts before starting them to ensure that they are safe.

- Tell workers to take additional precautions and exercise extra care when operating around power lines.

- Teach workers that outriggers on mobile cranes must rest on firm ground, on timbers, or be sufficiently cribbed to spread the weight of the crane and the load over a large enough area.   (Some mobile cranes cannot operate with outriggers in the traveling position.)

- Direct workers to always keep hoisting chains and ropes free of kinks or twists and never wrapped around a load.

- Train workers to attach loads to the load hook by slings, fixtures, and other devices that have the capacity to support the load on the hook.

- Instruct workers to pad sharp edges of loads to prevent cutting slings.

- Teach workers to maintain proper sling angles so that slings are not loaded in excess of their capacity.

- Ensure that all cranes are inspected frequently by persons thoroughly familiar with the crane, the methods of inspecting the crane, and what can make the crane unserviceable. Crane activity, the severity of use, and environmental conditions should determine inspection schedules.

- Ensure that the critical parts of a crane—such as crane operating mechanisms, hooks, air, or hydraulic system components and other load-carrying components—are inspected daily for any maladjustment, deterioration, leakage, deformation, or other damage.

What must employers do to ensure the safe use of slings?

As an employer, you must designate a competent person to conduct inspections of slings before and during use, especially when service conditions warrant. In addition, you must ensure that workers observe the following precautions when working with slings:

- Remove immediately damaged or defective slings from service.

- Do not shorten slings with knots or bolts or other makeshift devices.

- Do not kink sling legs.

- Do not load slings beyond their rated capacity.

- Keep suspended loads clear of all obstructions.

- Remain clear of loads about to be lifted and suspended.

- Do not engage in shock loading.

- Avoid sudden crane acceleration and deceleration when moving suspended loads.

What must employers do to protect workers who operate powered industrial trucks?

Workers who handle and store materials often use fork trucks, platform lift trucks, motorized hand trucks, and other specialized industrial trucks powered by electrical motors or internal combustion engines. Employers must make these workers aware of the safety requirements pertaining the design, maintenance, and use of these trucks.

What are the safety requirements for design?

All new powered industrial trucks, except vehicles intended primarily for earth moving or over-the-road hauling, must meet the design and construction requirements for powered industrial trucks established in the *American National Standard for Powered Industrial Trucks, Part II,* ANSI B56.1-1969. Trucks approved for fire safety also must bear a label, or some other identifying mark, indicating acceptance by a nationally recognized testing laboratory.

What are the safety requirements for modification?

You and your employees must not make modifications and additions affecting capacity and safe operation of the trucks without the manufacturer's prior written approval. In these cases, you must change capacity, operation, and maintenance instruction plates and tags or decals to reflect the new information. If the truck is equipped with front-end attachments that are not factory installed, the user must request that the truck be marked to identify these attachments and show the truck's approximate weight—including the installed attachment—when it is at maximum elevation with its load laterally centered.

What are the safety requirements for designation?

There are 11 different designations of industrial trucks, and each designation is suitable for use in certain locations and under specific conditions. Workers must not use powered industrial trucks in atmospheres containing hazardous concentrations of the following substances:

- Acetylene
- Butadiene

- Acetaldehyde
- Cyclopropane
- Ethylene
- Isoprene
- Hydrogen (or gases or vapors equivalent in hazard to hydrogen)
- Ethylene oxide
- Propylene oxide
- Diethyl ether
- Unsymmetrical dimethyl hydrazine

In addition, workers may not use these trucks in atmospheres containing hazardous concentrations of metal dust, including aluminum, magnesium, and other metals of similarly hazardous characteristics. In atmospheres containing carbon black, coal, or coke dust, workers may use only approved powered industrial trucks designated as EX. Where dusts of magnesium, aluminum, or bronze may be present, fuses, switches, motor controllers, and circuit breakers of trucks must have enclosures specifically approved for such locations.

Some powered industrial trucks are designed, constructed, and assembled for use in atmospheres containing flammable vapors or dusts. These include powered industrial trucks equipped with the following:

- Additional safeguards to their exhaust, fuel, and electrical systems;
- No electrical equipment (including the ignition);
- Temperature limitation features; and
- Electric motors and all other electrical equipment completely enclosed.

Workers may use these specially designed powered industrial trucks in locations where volatile flammable liquids or flammable gases are handled, processed, or used. The liquids, vapors, or gases should be confined within closed containers or closed systems and not allowed to escape. These trucks are approved and generally designated as DS, DY, ES, EE, EX, GS, or LPS. See Title 29 of the *Code of Federal Regulations (CFR)* Part 1910.178(b) for more detail on these designations.

What safety precautions should employers and workers observe when operating or maintaining powered industrial trucks?

When operating or maintaining powered industrial trucks, you and your employees must consider the following safety precautions:

- Fit high-lift rider trucks with an overhead guard if permitted by operating conditions.

- Equip fork trucks with vertical load backrest extensions according to manufacturers' specifications if the load presents a hazard.

- Locate battery-charging installations in designated areas.

- Provide facilities for flushing and neutralizing spilled electrolytes when changing or recharging batteries to prevent fires, to protect the charging apparatus from being damaged by the trucks, and to adequately ventilate fumes in the charging area from gassing batteries.

- Provide conveyor, overhead hoist, or equivalent materials handling equipment for handling batteries.

- Provide auxiliary directional lighting on the truck where general lighting is less than 2 lumens per square foot.

- Do not place arms and legs between the uprights of the mast or outside the running lines of the truck.

- Set brakes and put other adequate protection in place to prevent movement of trucks, trailers, or railroad cars when using powered industrial trucks to load or unload materials onto them.

- Provide sufficient headroom under overhead installations, lights, pipes, and sprinkler systems.

- Provide personnel on the loading platform with the means to shut off power to the truck whenever a truck is equipped with vertical only (or vertical and horizontal) controls elevatable with the lifting carriage or forks for lifting personnel.

- Secure dockboards or bridge plates properly so they won't move when equipment moves over them.

- Handle only stable or safely arranged loads.

- Exercise caution when handling tools.

- Disconnect batteries before repairing electrical systems on trucks.

- Ensure that replacement parts on industrial trucks are equivalent to the original ones.

Are there any training requirements for operators of powered industrial trucks?

Yes. Effective March 1, 1999, employers must develop a training program specific to the type of truck to be driven and the working conditions encountered. Employers must also evaluate the operator's performance in the workplace and certify that each operator has successfully received the training needed. The certification must include the name of the operator, the date of training, the date of evaluation, and the identity of the person(s) performing the training or evaluation. In addition, you must conduct an evaluation of each powered industrial truck operator's performance at least once every 3 years.

You must also conduct such an evaluation as well as refresher training if one of the following applies:

- Operator is observed operating the vehicle in an unsafe manner;

- Operator is involved in an accident or near-miss incident;

- Operator receives an evaluation revealing unsafe operation of the truck;

- Operator is assigned to drive a different type of truck; or

- Condition in the workplace changes in a manner that could affect safe operation of the truck.

For more information contact your Regional OSHA office or visit our website at http://www.osha.gov/dte/library/ materials_library.html#poweredindustrialtrucks
For more detailed information on powered industrial trucks, overhead and gantry cranes, and slings, see 29 CFR Part 1910.178 through 1910.184 Subpart N.

Basic Safety and Health Principles

Employers can reduce injuries resulting from handling and storing materials by using some basic safety procedures such as adopting sound ergonomics practices, taking general fire safety precautions, and keeping aisles and passageways clear.

What Is Ergonomics?

Ergonomics is defined as the study of work and is based on the principle that the job should be adapted to fit the person rather than forcing the person to fit the job. Ergonomics focuses on the work environment, such as its design and function, as well as items—such as the design and function of work stations, controls, displays, safety devices, tools, and lighting to fit the employees' physical requirements and to ensure their health and well being.

Ergonomics includes restructuring or changing workplace conditions, to make the job easier, and reducing stressors that cause musculoskeletal disorders. In the area of materials handling and storing, ergonomic principles may require controls such as reducing the size or weight of the objects lifted, installing a mechanical lifting aid, or changing the height of a pallet or shelf.

Although no approach completely eliminates back injuries resulting from lifting materials, you can prevent a substantial number of lifting injuries by implementing an effective ergonomics program and by training your employees in appropriate lifting techniques.

What About Fire Safety?

In adhering to fire safety precautions, instruct employees that flammable and combustible materials must be stored according to their fire characteristics. Flammable liquids, for example, must be separated from other material by a fire wall. Also, other combustibles must be stored in an area where smoking and using an open flame or a spark-producing device is prohibited. Dissimilar materials that are dangerous when they come into contact with each other must be stored apart.

What About Aisles and Passageways?

When using aisles and passageways to move materials mechanically, workers must allow sufficient clearance for aisles at loading docks, through doorways, wherever turns must be made, and in other parts of the workplace. Providing sufficient clearance for mechanically-moved materials will prevent workers from being pinned between the equipment and fixtures in the workplace, such as walls, racks, posts, or other machines. Sufficient clearance also will prevent the load from striking an obstruction and falling on an employee.

Employers must ensure that all passageways that workers use remain clear of obstructions and tripping hazards. Workers should not store materials in excess of supplies needed for immediate operations in aisles or passageways, and employers must mark permanent aisles and passageways appropriately.

Training and Education

OSHA recommends that employers establish a formal training program to teach workers how to recognize and avoid materials handling hazards. Instructors should be well-versed in safety engineering and materials handling and storing. The training should reduce workplace hazards by emphasizing the following factors:

- Dangers of lifting without proper training.

- Avoidance of unnecessary physical stress and strain.

- Awareness of what a worker can comfortably handle without undue strain.

- Use of equipment properly.

- Recognition of potential hazards and how to prevent or correct them.

Should the prevention of some injuries receive special emphasis?

Yes. Because of the high incidence of back injuries, both supervisors and employees should demonstrate and practice safe manual lifting techniques. Training programs on proper lifting techniques should cover the following topics:

- Health risks of improper lifting, citing organizational case histories, vs the benefits of proper lifting.

- Basic anatomy of the spine, muscles, and joints of the trunk, and the contributions of intra-abdominal pressure while lifting.

- Body strengths and weaknesses—determining one's own lifting capacity.

- Physical factors that might contribute to an accident and how to avoid the unexpected.

- Safe postures for lifting and timing for smooth, easy lifting.

- Aids such as stages, platforms, or steps, trestles, shoulder pads, handles, and wheels.

- Body responses—warning signals—to be aware of when lifting.

How can employers make their training programs more effective?

To have an effective safety and health program covering materials handling and storing, your managers must take an active role in its development. You must convince first-line supervisors of the importance of controlling hazards associated with materials handling and storing and hold them accountable for employee training. An ongoing safety and health management system can motivate employees to continue using necessary protective gear and observing proper job procedures. Instituting such a program, along with providing the correct materials handling equipment, can enhance worker safety and health in the area of materials handling and storing. More training information is located a thttp://www.osha.gov/dsg/topics/safetyhealth/index html. For more help, contact the OSHA Training Institute or the regional or area office nearest to you. (See "How Can OSHA Help Me?" at the end of this booklet.)

OSHA Assistance

OSHA can provide extensive help through a variety of programs, including technical assistance about effective safety and health programs, state plans, workplace consultations, voluntary protection programs, strategic partnerships, and training and education, and more. Safety and health add value to your business, to your work, and to your life.

What are safety and health system management guidelines?

Effective management of worker safety and health protection is a decisive factor in reducing the extent and severity of work-related injuries and illnesses and their related costs. In fact, an effective safety and health program forms the basis of good worker protection and can save time and money–about $4 for every dollar spent–and increase productivity.

To assist employers and employees in developing effective safety and health programs, OSHA published recommended *Safety and Health Program Management Guidelines (Federal Register* 54(16): 3904-3916, January 26, 1989). These voluntary guidelines can be applied to all places of employment covered by OSHA.

The guidelines identify four general elements that are critical to the development of a successful safety and health management system:

- Management leadership and employee involvement,

- Worksite analysis,

- Hazard prevention and control, and

- Safety and health training.

The guidelines recommend specific actions, under each of these general elements, to achieve an effective safety and health program. The *Federal Register* notice is available online at **www.osha.gov**.

What are state programs?

The *Occupational Safety and Health Act of 1970 (OSH Act)* encourages states to develop and operate their own job safety and health plans. OSHA approves and monitors these plans. There are currently 26 state plans: 23 cover both private and public (state and local government) employment; 3 states, Connecticut, New Jersey, and New York, cover the public sector only. States and territories with their own OSHA-approved occupational safety and health plans must adopt standards identical to, or at least as effective as, the federal standards.

How do I obtain consultation services?

Consultation assistance is available on request to employers who want help in establishing and maintaining a safe and healthful workplace. Largely funded by OSHA, the service is provided at no cost to the employer. Primarily developed for smaller employers with more hazardous operations, the consultation service is delivered by state governments employing professional safety and health consultants. Comprehensive assistance includes an appraisal of all mechanical systems, work practices, and occupational safety and health hazards of the workplace and all aspects of the employer's present job safety and health program. In addition, the service offers assistance to employers in developing and implementing an effective safety and health program. No penalties are proposed or citations issued for hazards identified by the consultant. OSHA provides consultation assistance to the employer with the assurance that his or her name and firm and any information about the workplace will not be routinely reported to OSHA enforcement staff.

Under the consultation program, certain exemplary employers may request participation in OSHA's Safety and Health Achievement Recognition Program (SHARP). Eligibility for participation in SHARP includes receiving a comprehensive consultation visit, demonstrating exemplary achievements in workplace safety and health by abating all identified hazards, and developing an excellent safety and health program.

Employers accepted into SHARP may receive an exemption from programmed inspections (not complaint or accident investigation inspections) for a period of 1 year. For more information concerning consultation assistance, see the list of consultation projects listed at the end of this publication.

What are Voluntary Protection Programs (VPPs)?

Voluntary Protection Programs and onsite consultation services, when coupled with an effective enforcement program, expand worker protection to help meet the goals of the *OSH Act*. The three VPPs—Star, Merit, and Demonstration—are designed to recognize outstanding achievements by companies that have successfully incorporated comprehensive safety and health programs into their total management system. The VPPs motivate others to achieve excellent safety and health results in the same outstanding way as they establish a cooperative relationship between employers, employees, and OSHA.

For additional information on VPPs and how to apply, contact the OSHA regional offices listed at the end of this publication.

What is the Strategic Partnership Program?

OSHA's Strategic Partnership Program, the newest member of OSHA's cooperative programs, helps encourage, assist, and recognize the efforts of partners to eliminate serious workplace hazards and achieve a high level of worker safety and health. Whereas OSHA's Consultation Program and VPP entail one-on-one relationships between OSHA and individual worksites, most strategic partnerships seek to have a broader impact by building cooperative relationships with groups of employers and employees. These partnerships are voluntary, cooperative relationships between OSHA, employers, employee representatives, and others (e.g., trade unions, trade and professional associations, universities, and other government agencies).

For more information on this program, contact your nearest OSHA office, or visit OSHA's website at **www.osha.gov**.

Does OSHA offer training and education?

OSHA's area offices offer a variety of information services, such as compliance assistance, technical advice, publications, audiovisual aids and speakers for special engagements. OSHA's Training Institute in Des Plaines, IL, provides basic and advanced courses in safety and health for federal and state compliance officers, state consultants, federal agency personnel, and private sector employers, employees, and their representatives.

The OSHA Training Institute also has established OSHA Training Institute Education Centers to address the increased demand for its courses from the private sector and from other federal agencies. These centers are nonprofit colleges, universities, and other organizations that have been selected after a competition for participation in the program.

OSHA also provides funds to nonprofit organizations, through grants, to conduct workplace training and education in subjects where OSHA believes there is a lack of workplace training. Grants are awarded annually. Grant recipients are expected to contribute 20 percent of the total grant cost.

For more information on grants, training, and education, contact the OSHA Training Institute, Office of Training and Education, 1555 Times Drive, Des Plaines, IL 60018, (847) 297-4810. For further information on any OSHA program, contact your nearest OSHA area or regional office listed at the end of this publication.

Does OSHA provide any information electronically?

OSHA has a variety of materials and tools available on its website–**www.osha.gov**. These include *e-Tools* such as *Expert Advisors, Electronic Compliance Assistance Tools (e-CATs), Technical Links;* regulations, directives, publications; videos, and other information for employers and employees. OSHA's software programs and compliance assistance tools walk you through challenging safety and health issues and common problems to find the best solutions for your workplace.

OSHA's CD-ROM includes standards, interpretations, directives, and more and can be purchased on CD-ROM from the U.S. Government Printing Office. To order, write to the Superintendent of Documents, P.O. Box 371954, Pittsburgh, PA 15250-7954 or phone (202) 512-1800. Specify OSHA Regulations, Documents and Technical Information on CD-ROM (ORDT), GPO Order No. S/N 729-013-00000-5. The price is $53 per year ($66.25 foreign); $15 per single copy ($18.75 foreign).

How do I learn more about related OSHA publications?

OSHA has an extensive publications program. For a listing of free or sales items, visit OSHA's website at **www.osha.gov** or contact the OSHA Publications Office , U.S. Department of Labor, OSHA/OSHA Publications, P.O. Box 37535, Washington, DC 20013-7535. Telephone (202) 693-1888 or fax to (202) 693-2498.

How do I contact OSHA about emergencies, complaints, or further assistance?

To report an emergency, file a complaint, or seek OSHA advice, assistance, or products, call 1-800-321-OSHA or contact your nearest OSHA regional or area office listed at the end of this publication. The teletypewriter (TTY) number is 1-877-889-5627.

You can also file a complaint online and obtain more information on OSHA federal and state programs by visiting OSHA's website at **www.osha.gov**.

For more information on grants, training, and education, contact the OSHA Training Institute, Office of Training and Education, 1555 Times Drive, Des Plaines, Il 60018, (847) 297-4810, or see **Outreach** on OSHA's website at **www.osha.gov**.

Glossary

Boom - A long, straight beam hinged at one end and used for lifting heavy objects by means of cables and/or hydraulics. Booms can be of lattice construction or be made of heavy tubular material.

Boom radius - The horizontal distance from the axis of rotation of a crane or derrick boom to the boom tip.

Bracing - A diagonal piece of structural material that serves to strengthen something.

Chassis - The frame upon which a vehicle's body is mounted.

Chock - A wedge or block for steadying a body and holding it motionless, for filling in excess space, or for preventing the movement of a wheel.

Competent person - one who can identify health and safety hazards in the workplace and has the authority to correct them.

Crib - To line or support with a framework of timber.

Cumulative trauma disorders - Injuries that result from continuous or repetitive motions over prolonged periods of time.

Outrigger - A projecting member that extends from a main structure to either provide additional stability or support.

Powered industrial trucks - Forklift trucks, tractors, platform lift trucks, motorized hand trucks, and other specialized industrialized trucks powered by electrical or internal combustion engines.

Rigger - A worker who prepares heavy equipment or loads of material for lifting.

Related Publications

Single free copies of the following publications can be obtained from the U.S. Department of Labor, OSHA/OSHA Publications Office, P.O. Box 37535, Washington, DC 20013-7535. Send a self-addressed mailing label with your request. Publications may also be ordered from **www.osha.gov**.

All About OSHA – OSHA 2056

Concrete and Masonry Construction – OSHA 3106

Consultation Services for the Employer – OSHA 3047

Control of Hazardous Energy (Lockout/Tagout) – OSHA 3120

Crane or Derrick Suspended Platforms – OSHA 3100

Personal Protective Equipment – OSHA 3077

Sling Safety – OSHA 3072

The following publications are available from the Superintendent of Documents, U.S. Government Printing Office, P.O Box 371954, Pittsburgh, PA 15250-7954. Phone orders: 1-866-512-1800 (toll free); 202-512-1800 (Metro DC). Or visit GPO online at www.gpo.gov/su_docs/ for current ordering and pricing information.

Assessing the Need for Personal Protective Equipment: A Guide for Small Business Employers (OSHA 3151).

Ergonomics: The Study of Work (OSHA 3125).

Handbook for Small Business (OSHA 2209).

Job Hazard Analysis (OSHA 3071).

Title 29 Code of Federal Regulations (*CFR*) Part 1900 to 1910.999 (General Industry Standards).

Title 29 Code of Federal Regulations (*CFR*) Part 1910.1000 to End (General Industry Standards).

Title 29 Code of Federal Regulations (*CFR*) Part 1926 (Construction)

OSHA Office Directory

OSHA Regional Offices

Region I

(CT,* ME, MA, NH, RI, VT*)
JFK Federal Building, Room E340
Boston, MA 02203
(617) 565-9860

Region II

(NJ,* NY,* PR,* VI*)
201 Varick Street, Room 670
New York, NY 10014
(212) 337-2378

Region III

(DE, DC, MD,* PA,* VA,* WV)
The Curtis Center
170 S. Independence Mall West
Suite 740 West
Philadelphia, PA 19106-3309
(215) 861-4900

Region IV

(AL, FL, GA, KY,* MS, NC,* SC,*
TN*)
SNAF
61 Forsyth Street SW, Room 6T50
Atlanta, GA 30303
(404) 562-2300

Region V

(IL, IN,* MI,* MN,* OH, WI)
230 South Dearborn Street,
Room 3244
Chicago, IL 60604
(312) 353-2220

Region VI

(AR, LA, NM,* OK, TX)
525 Griffin Street, Room 602
Dallas, TX 75202
(214) 767-4731 or 4736 x224

Region VII

(IA,* KS, MO, NE)
City Center Square
1100 Main Street, Suite 800
Kansas City, MO 64105
(816) 426-5861

Region VIII

(CO, MT, ND, SD, UT,* WY*)
1999 Broadway, Suite 1690
PO Box 46550
Denver, CO 80202-5716
(303) 844-1600

Region IX

(American Samoa, AZ,* CA,* HI,
NV,* Northern Mariana Islands)
71 Stevenson Street, Room 420
San Francisco, CA 94105
(415) 975-4310

Region X

(AK,* ID, OR,* WA*)
1111 Third Avenue, Suite 715
Seattle, WA 98101-3212
(206) 553-5930

*These states and territories operate their own OSHA-approved job safety and health programs (Connecticut, New Jersey and New York plans cover public employees only). States with approved programs must have a standard that is identical to, or at least as effective as, the federal standard.

OSHA Area Offices

Birmingham, AL .... (205) 731-1534
Mobile, AL .... (251) 441-6131
Anchorage, AK .... (907) 271-5152
Little Rock, AR .... (501) 324-6291(5818)
Phoenix, AZ .... (602) 640-2348
San Diego, CA .... (619) 557-5909
Sacramento, CA .... (916) 566-7471
Denver, CO .... (303) 844-5285
Greenwood Village, CO .... (303) 843-4500
Bridgeport, CT .... (203) 579-5581
Hartford, CT .... (860) 240-3152
Wilmington, DE .... (302) 573-6518
Fort Lauderdale, FL .... (954) 424-0242
Jacksonville, FL .... (904) 232-2895
Tampa, FL .... (813) 626-1177
Savannah, GA .... (912) 652-4393
Smyrna, GA .... (770) 984-8700
Tucker, GA .... (770) 493-6644/6742/8419
Des Moines, IA .... (515) 284-4794
Boise, ID .... (208) 321-2960
Calumet City, IL .... (708) 891-3800
Des Plaines, IL .... (847) 803-4800
Fairview Heights, IL .... (618) 632-8612
North Aurora, IL .... (630) 896-8700
Peoria, IL .... (309) 671-7033
Indianapolis, IN .... (317) 226-7290
Wichita, KS .... (316) 269-6644
Frankfort, KY .... (502) 227-7024
Baton Rouge, LA .... (225) 389-0474 (0431)
Braintree, MA .... (617) 565-6924
Methuen, MA .... (617) 565-8110
Springfield, MA .... (413) 785-0123
Linthicum, MD .... (410) 865-2055/2056
Bangor, ME .... (207) 941-8177
Portland, ME .... (207) 780-3178

August, ME	(207) 622-8417
Lansing, MI	(517) 327-0904
Minneapolis, MN	(612) 664- 5460
Kansas City, MO	(816) 483-9531
St. Louis, MO	(314) 425-4249
Jackson, MS	(601) 965-4606
Billings, MT	(406) 247-7494
Raleigh, NC	(919) 856-4770
Omaha, NE	(402) 221-3182
Bismark, ND	(701) 250-4521
Concord, NH	(603) 225-1629
Avenel, NJ	(732) 750-3270
Hasbrouck Heights, NJ	(201) 288-1700
Marlton, NJ	(856) 757-5181
Parsippany, NJ	(973) 263-1003
Carson City, NV	(775) 885-6963
Albany, NY	(518) 464-4338
Bayside, NY	(718) 279-9060
Bowmansville, NY	(716) 684-3891
New York, NY	(212) 337-2636
North Syracuse, NY	(315) 451-0808
Tarrytown, NY	(914) 524-7510
Westbury, NY	(516) 334-3344
Cincinnati, OH	(513) 841-4132
Cleveland, OH	(216) 522-3818
Columbus, OH	(614) 469-5582
Toledo, OH	(419) 259-7542
Oklahoma City, OK	(405) 278-9560
Portland, OR	(503) 326-2251
Allentown, PA	(610) 776-0592
Erie, PA	(814) 833-5758
Harrisburg, PA	(717) 782-3902
Philadelphia, PA	(215) 597-4955
Pittsburgh, PA	(412) 395-4903
Wilkes-Barre, PA	(570) 826-6538
Guaynabo, PR	(787) 277-1560
Providence, RI	(401) 528-4669

OSHA-Approved State Plans

Commissioner
Alaska Department of Labor
1111 W. 8th Street, Room 308
P.O. Box 21149
Juneau, AK   99802-1149
(907) 465-2700

Director
Industrial Commission of Arizona
800 W. Washington
Phoenix, AZ   85007
(602) 542-5795

Director
California Department of
Industrial Relations
455 Golden Gate Avenue -
10th floor
San Francisco, CA   94102
(415) 703-5050

Commissioner
Connecticut Department of Labor
200 Folly Brook Boulevard
Wethersfield, CT   06109
(860) 263-6505

Director
Hawaii Department of Labor and
Industrial Relations
830 Punchbowl Street
Honolulu, HI   96831
(808) 586-8844

Commissioner
Iowa Division of Labor
1000 E. Grand Avenue
Des Moines, IA   50319
(515) 281-3447

Commissioner
Indiana Department of Labor
State Office Building
402 West Washington Street -
Room W195
Indianapolis, IN   46204
(317) 232-2378

Secretary
Kentucky Labor Cabinet
1047 U.S. Highway 127 South,
Suite 4
Frankfort, KY   40601
(502) 564-3070

Commissioner
Maryland Division of Labor and
Industry
Department of Labor Licensing and
Regulation
MOSH
1100 N. Eutaw Street, Room 613
Baltimore, MD   21201-2206
(410) 767-2215

Director
Michigan Department of
Consumer and Industry Services
P.O. Box 30643
7150 Harris Drive
Lansing, MI   48909
(517) 373-7230

Commissioner
Minnesota Department of Labor
and Industry
443 Lafayette Road
St. Paul, MN   55155
(651) 284-5010

Commissioner
North Carolina Department of
Labor
4 West Edenton Street
Raleigh, NC 27601-1092
(919) 807-2900

Commissioner
New Jersey Department of Labor
John Fitch Plaza - Labor Building
Market and Warren Streets
P.O. Box 110
Trenton, NJ 08625-0110
(609) 292-2975

Secretary
New Mexico Environment
Department
1190 St. Francis Drive
P.O. Box 26110
Santa Fe, NM 87502
(505) 827-2850

Commissioner
New York Department of Labor
W. Averell Harriman State Office
Building-12, Room 500
Albany, NY 12240
(518) 457-2741

Administrator
Nevada Division of Industrial
Relations
400 West King Street, Suite 400
Carson City, NV 89703
(775) 684–7260

Administrator
Oregon Department of Consumer
and Business Services
Occupational Safety and Health
Division (OR-OSHA)
350 Winter Street, N.E. Room 430
Salem, OR 97310-3882
(503) 378-3272

Secretary
Puerto Rico Department of Labor
and Human Resources
Prudencio Rivera Martinez Building
505 Munoz Rivera Avenue
Hato Rey, PR 00918
(787) 754-2119

Director
South Carolina Department of
Labor, Licensing and Regulation
Koger Office Park, Kingstree
Building
110 Centerview Drive
P.O. Box 11329
Columbia, SC 29211
(803) 896-4300

Commissioner
Tennessee Department of Labor
and Workforce Development
710 James Robertson Parkway
Andrew Johnson Tower
Nashville, TN 37243-0659
(615) 741-2582

Commissioner
Labor Commission of Utah
160 East 300 South Street,
3rd floor
P.O. Box 146650
Salt Lake City, UT 84111
(801) 530-6901

Commissioner
Virginia Department of Labor and
Industry
Powers-Taylor Building
13 South 13th Street
Richmond, VA 23219
(804) 786-2377

Commissioner
Virgin Islands Department of Labor
2203 Church Street
Christiansted, St. Croix, VI
00820-4660
(340) 773-1990

Commissioner
Vermont Department of Labor and
Industry
National Life Building—Drawer 20
120 State Street
Montpelier VT 05620-3401
(802) 828-2288

Director
Washington Department of Labor
and Industries
P.O. Box 44001
Olympia, WA 98504-4001
(360) 902-4200
(360) 902-5430

Administrator
Worker's Safety and Compensation
 Division (WSC)
Wyoming Department of
Employment
Herschler Building, 2nd Floor East
122 West 25th Street
Cheyenne, WY 82002
(307) 777-7786

OSHA Consultation Projects

Anchorage, AK .... (907) 269-4957

Tuscaloosa, AL .... (205) 348-3033

Little Rock, AR .... (501) 682-4522

Phoenix, AZ .... (602) 542-1695

Sacramento, CA .... (916) 263-2856

Fort Collins, CO .... (970) 491-6151

Wethersfield, CT .... (860) 566-4550

Washington, DC .... (202) 541-3727

Wilmington, DE .... (302) 761-8219

Tampa, FL .... (813) 974-9962

Atlanta, GA .... (404) 894-2643

Tiyam, GU .... 9-1-(671) 475-1101

Honolulu, HI .... (808) 586-9100

Des Moines, IA .... (515) 281-7629

Boise, ID .... (208) 426-3283

Chicago, IL .... (312) 814-2337

Indianapolis, IN .... (317) 232-2688

Topeka, KS .... (785) 296-2251

Frankfort, KY .... (502) 564-6895

Baton Rouge, LA .... (225) 342-9601

West Newton, MA .... (617) 727-3982

Laurel, MD .... (410) 880-4970

Augusta, ME .... (207) 624-6400

Lansing, MI .... (517) 322-1809

Saint Paul, MN .... (651) 284-5060

Jefferson City, MO .... (573) 751-3403

Pearl, MS .... (601) 939-2047

Helena, MT .... (406) 444-6418

Raleigh, NC .... (919) 807-2905

Bismarck, ND .... (701) 328-5188

Lincoln, NE .... (402) 471-4717

Concord, NH .... (603) 271-2024

Trenton, NJ .... (609) 292-3923

Santa Fe, NM .... (505) 827-4230

Albany, NY .... (518) 457-2238
Henderson, NV .... (702) 486-9140
Columbus, OH .... (614) 644-2631
Oklahoma City, OK .... (405) 528-1500
Salem, OR .... (503) 378-3272
Indiana, PA .... (724) 357-2396
Hato Rey, PR .... (787) 754-2171
Providence, RI .... (401) 222-2438
Columbia, SC .... (803) 734-9614
Brookings, SD .... (605) 688-4101
Nashville, TN .... (615) 741-7036
Austin, TX .... (512) 804-4640
Salt Lake City, UT .... (801) 530-6901
Montpelier, VT .... (802) 828-2765
Richmond, VA .... (804) 786-6359
Christiansted St. Croix, VI .... (809) 772-1315
Olympia, WA .... (360) 902-5638
Madison, WI .... (608) 266-9383
Waukesha, WI .... (262) 523-3044
Charleston, WV .... (304) 558-7890
Cheyenne, WY .... (307) 777-7786